# INTEGRITYW⚙RKS

## TOOLS AND SKILLS TO BUILD INTEGRITY

# ROY J. SNELL

SCCE™
Society of Corporate
Compliance and Ethics

# Praise for *IntegrityWorks*

*"In* IntegrityWorks, *Roy Snell achieves the difficult but invaluable objective of providing inspiration as well as a set of practical frameworks, questions, and tools to support the pursuit of integrity in our professional and everyday lives. Rather than preaching, he skillfully weaves together personal stories, interviews with exemplary leaders, and insights from research to feed and enable our already existing aspirations toward authenticity. This is a profoundly readable, practical, empowering, and enabling book for all of us who would like to bring our whole and best selves to our professional endeavors."*
**—Mary C. Gentile, PhD, Author of Giving Voice To Values: How To Speak Your Mind When You Know What's Right *and professor of practice at University of Virginia Darden School of Business***

*"Authentic, high-integrity leaders have the ability to inspire those around them and help those people achieve more than they thought possible. At the root of this inspiration is that these leaders encourage those around them to be their authentic 'best selves' as often as possible. Roy Snell's book provides very helpful, practical advice for leaders about how to enhance their effectiveness along these important dimensions."*
**—Tim Welsh, former Sr. Partner at McKinsey and current Vice Chair of Consumer & Business Banking at US Bank**

"*I am sure that* IntegrityWorks *will be a favorite among Panamanian professionals. It has everything you need—it is fun, useful, and most importantly, it helps you think differently.*"
**—Dr. Carlos Barsallo, President, Board of Directors at Transparency International Panama**

"*I am so grateful for this book . . . it provides a logical framework to organize observations and data to assess whether further discussion and investigation is needed for a compliance activity.*"
**—Andra M. Popa, Compliance Specialist**

"*Bound to initiate plenty of heated discussions about ethics, integrity, and related subjects. Roy's done his research and applies it excellently to real-life issues of integrity, never losing sight of how a lack of integrity manifests itself and gets in the way of so many things we do on a daily basis.*"
**—Gerry Zack, CEO of Society of Corporate Compliance and Ethics & Health Care Compliance Association**

*IntegrityWorks: Tools and Skills to Build Integrity* is published by the Society of Corporate Compliance and Ethics, Minneapolis, MN.

ISBN 978-1-7335987-0-5

*Editor*: Karen Latchana Kenney
*Designer*: Craig Micke

This publication is designed to provide accurate, comprehensive and authoritative information on the subject matter covered. However, the publisher does not warrant that information contained herein is complete or accurate. This book is published with the understanding that the publisher is not engaged in rendering legal or other professional services. If legal advice or other expert assistance is required, the services of a competent professional should be sought.

**Society of Corporate Compliance and Ethics**
6500 Barrie Road, Suite 250
Minneapolis, MN 55435

p +1 952 933 4977 or 888 277 4977 | f +1 952 988 0146

corporatecompliance.org | helpteam@corporatecompliance.org

# DEDICATION

I dedicate this book to my family who helped me with my integrity. One of my greatest hopes is that my daughters have integrity throughout their entire lives; because if they do . . . I know they will be happy.

# ACKNOWLEDGMENTS

My sincere thanks go to Margaret Hambleton, Dan Roach, Gerry Zack, and Joel A. Rogers for agreeing to be interviewed for this book and for their meaningful contributions on this important topic. They are amongst the most amazing of many amazing compliance and ethics professionals that I have had the opportunity to work with over the past 23 years.

I appreciate Karen Latchana Kenney's editorial work developing this book. Her help is beyond description.

Many thanks to Brian Back, who not only provided the foreword, but also sat with me many times to discuss and brainstorm topics for this book. His advice was focused and logical, which helped me describe integrity in a practical way that everyone can understand and implement in their daily lives.

# CONTENTS

# FOREWORD

When Roy asked me to lunch and told me about his idea for this book, I knew it would be a really complex topic to write about. But I thought, *Roy is the right person to take this on*. He has the unique ability to cut through complex topics and provide clear and concise summaries and thoughts.

My relationship with Roy began about six years ago when he hired me to help him find a CFO . . . and then several more searches followed. For 25 years I have evaluated candidates—well over 1,000—as an executive recruiter. Through all those years and interactions, I've noticed an indelible arc to the behavioral patterns of the candidates and clients I have interacted with. The erosion of integrity has not been dramatic or instant, but like all erosion, it's been slow and steady . . . and undeniable. What is fascinating is *why* I think this is happening: you cannot listen to a TV show, a newscast, or political discourse today without observing a significant amount of spin, manipulation, and even deceit. And this is done at the expense of truth and transparency.

Roy and I had several lunches and follow-up discussions on integrity. We bounced ideas off each other, and I could see his passion for this topic. We talked about where integrity comes from and whether there are objective standards to benchmark all behavior. We discussed people we knew who exemplified high degrees of integrity, while also acknowledging that we all have missteps along the way. One of the most fascinating aspects of the discussions was about the idea of effecting change in our culture. It was clear Roy had been thinking about integrity for a long time, and this book would be the sum of all his thoughts.

I'll leave you with this short anecdote that I think describes Roy's relationship with integrity. I was rebuilding my business website and asked Roy if he would be willing to share his experience working with me for the site. Ten minutes later I received his reply. Thinking he was letting me know he'd get back to me, I was surprised to see he had already written something. It wasn't simply a nice comment or a single sentence—it was a detailed paragraph of his personal opinions about my service and approach. I responded with my gratitude and surprise at how fast he turned that around. His reply? "The truth is fast and easy to come by; it's people that produce BS who take a little longer."

**Brian Back**
**December, 2019**

# Introduction

# WHY INTEGRITY?

"Integrity isn't just doing the right thing when no one is looking. Integrity is doing the unpopular but right thing when the pressure is on and everyone is looking."
—*Gerry Zack, SCCE & HCCA CEO*

"Somebody once said that in looking for people to hire, you look for three qualities: integrity, intelligence, and energy. And if you don't have the first, the other two will kill you. You think about it; it's true. If you hire somebody without [integrity], you really want them to be dumb and lazy."[1]
—*Warren E. Buffett, Berkshire Hathaway CEO*

Could you believe in a leader with unlimited charisma but who never keeps her word? Would you question the work of an employee who's known to tell many small, somewhat harmless lies? Or could you trust the advice of a friend who doesn't critically question the information he reads? Each of these circumstances brings up the question of a person's integrity—being honest, measured and fair in thought, and true to one's personal values. If you don't act with integrity, you will have trouble getting people to believe in you. Few people with integrity will follow or trust you. And you will never be an effective leader, reliable friend, or trusted advisor. It simply kills your character and reputation.

Every person encounters situations both professionally and personally that test their integrity. It's inevitable, and it will undoubtedly happen throughout your lifetime. It's something I've experienced and seen happen to many compliance and ethics professionals—people who dedicate their careers to promoting and defending ethical behavior. On a daily basis, for example, they have to assess whether or not an accusation against an employee has merit and needs to be investigated, or if it's just some form of character assassination. And if an accusation does end up being true, they need to have the courage to confront the situation head-on for the benefit of the company as a whole. They have to make ethical decisions like these, even if powerful people's reputations will be damaged. Compliance and ethics professionals do this often in their careers, but these kinds of ethical situations come up in every organization and in every field, and we all confront difficult circumstances like these in our daily lives.

Acting according to your beliefs may not always be the easiest choice to make, and it may make you a few enemies too. But if you want to be trusted, respected, and believed, acting with integrity is the only choice you have. It's critical in business decisions, and it's vital within personal relationships.

**ROY-ISM**

Every human needs a little compliance and ethics professional in them.

Some of the words are dated or a bit odd, I know. These words will help you avoid the trap that many people fall into when they say: "Think like me politically, socially, and managerially and you will have integrity too." When someone talks about integrity in a similar way, or you are tempted to use a similar approach, think back to these words . . . none of which exhibit such personal views. Originally, I told my editor, Karen, that I was going to delete the odd ones. She asked, "So you are going to biasedly pick the ones that serve your purpose and leave out the ones that don't?" *I put all the words in the book.* Bias is everywhere . . . even in a book about integrity.

## Testing My Integrity

One of the first situations that tested my integrity happened when I was around 10 years old . . . as best as I can remember anyway. I was in Southdale Center, a shopping mall in Edina, Minnesota, with the distinction of being the first indoor mall in the United States. Prior to that moment, the most dishonest thing I had done was search my father's pockets for spare change, which I figured he didn't need or wouldn't miss.

That moment at Southdale made an impression on me. I'll never forget it. My friend and I were into building model cars at the time, and for whatever reason, we decided to steal from the hobby store. I shoved some paint brushes up my coat sleeve. I do not recall what my buddy took, but I do remember watching an adult catch him doing it. So I did what any good friend with stolen merchandise up his sleeve would do . . . *I quickly left the store.*

I waited outside for what seemed like an eternity. There is no peace of mind during moments like that one . . . and it still haunts me 54 years later. I think it bothers me more that I walked out on my buddy than the fact that I stole something. My friend finally came out and told me the employee said he had to wait for the manager, but the manager never came and my friend was let go.

And that was the brilliance of the employee: *there was no manager coming.* The guy wanted to leave an impression on a 10-year-old boy. He could have called his parents and ensured more suffering, but the man thought the torture of waiting would be enough. He was right. Not only did it work for my friend, it worked for another 10-year-old thief waiting just outside the store—me.

We all have lapses in judgment, and my conscience haunts me mercilessly after my lapses in judgment. This event is a good example of that. *Your conscience is one of the best guardians of your integrity.*

## Thoughts on Integrity: Barack Obama

In an October 2019 Obama Foundation Summit panel discussion, President Barack Obama described his personal journey to becoming the person he wanted to become— someone who could effect change in society—and having integrity was an important part of that journey:

❝ For me, at least, it was not a straight line . . . it was an evolution that took place over time as I tried to align what I believed most deeply with what I saw around me and with my own actions. . . . [it] was this long process for me of aligning what I said I believed in with my behavior and then testing what I could change so that the world would align better with what I believed in and my values.

So the first stage is just kind of figuring out—alright, what do you really believe? What's really important to you? Not what you pretend is important to you, but what is really important to you? And what are you willing to risk or sacrifice for it? The next phase is then you test that against the world, and the world kicks you in the teeth, and says: 'You may think this is important, but you know what? We've got other ideas. And who are you? And you can't change nothing.' And then you get through a phase of trying to develop skills and courage and resilience and you try to fit your actions to the scale of whatever influence you have . . . and that gives you the power to then analyze and say here's what worked, here's what didn't, here's what I need more of in order to achieve the vision and the goals that I have.[2] ❞

## Growing Your Integrity

So how do you act with integrity? And how do you help it grow? We can learn about having integrity from observing how our family, friends, and colleagues act. But the real journey begins within, by understanding what your personal values are, how you process information, and how you can have the courage to act in accordance with your beliefs. And you need to view it as a process, something you have to work on daily in order to maintain. It's not just in the actions you learn to take, it's in the convictions you hold for your entire life.

Authenticity, honesty, truth, critical thinking, and bias—these are just some aspects of integrity I discuss in the chapters of this book that can give you the tools to make better, more measured decisions. You'll see that by talking with experts, sharing experiences, practicing honest self-reflection, and applying new skills to new contexts, you can build personal, team, and organizational integrity. Through quotes, definitions, and charts, you'll get a better understanding of what the somewhat enigmatic concept of "integrity" really means. And through the "Now You Try" workshop exercises, you can put some of these ideas into practice to see what works or doesn't work for you.

Also in each chapter, you'll find an interview with someone I consider to be an ethical superstar—Joel A. Rogers, Gerry Zack, Dan Roach, and Margaret Hambleton. Most are responsible for the ethics of a very large organization with tens of thousands of employees or members. They each contribute a unique and different perspective to the chapter's topic. I believe other people can help you on this journey, which I learned from my mentor, Marc Dettmann. Consulting people who have been through what you are going through is one of the best habits you can develop to grow both personally and professionally.

Building your integrity is not an easy process—it's complicated and sometimes difficult. In order to succeed, you need to value it more than almost anything else—more than power, recognition, and money. You have to be in it for the long haul, but it's entirely possible and entirely worth the work. This book can help you do that work in different ways. Use it to start ethics discussions with friends or employees. Try it in a mentor-mentee relationship to spark meaningful conversations. Use the exercises in workshops to start conquering biases and thinking critically when making decisions. This book is just a starting point—try some skills and tools I suggest and then develop your own. So let's get started by working on personal honesty—a quality to build a strong foundation of integrity upon.

# Chapter 1

# THE GREATEST HONESTY IS TO OURSELVES

———————

"Don't let the noise of others' opinions drown out your own inner voice. And most important, have the courage to follow your heart and intuition. They somehow already know what you truly want to become."[1]
—*Steve Jobs, cofounder and former Apple Inc. CEO*

When I told Vinca Russell, senior manager of global ethics & compliance communications, training, and initiatives at Ingersoll Rand, that I was writing a book on integrity, she said it got her "thinking about a few things in my life. Mainly being honest with myself . . . we so often think about honesty as it relates to what we say and do to/for *others*. The greatest honesty, in my humble opinion, is to *ourselves*."[2]

Of all the things she could have said about integrity, she had no idea that I consider this idea to be so important. She had no idea that I feel we have to work on honesty within ourselves before we can have integrity with others. She, in my humble opinion, hit the nail on the head. If we are not honest with ourselves, we cannot understand what our core beliefs are and make decisions that adhere to them. We cannot be authentic in our lives and we cannot be honest with others.

## Cultures and Norms

Being authentic helps you make more measured and balanced decisions that align to your beliefs. This benefits your personal life as well as your professional life. Yet many organizational cultures beg you to be someone else, expecting you to conform to their ideal behavior, thinking, or norms. Large organizations, especially, often have strict rules about "what is acceptable to say or do here." During my almost 40 years of managing people, I struggled with this too. Eventually, I realized that people were often more productive if they were left to just be themselves. Some managers really don't know how to run a business, so they micromanage their employees and focus on minutia and policies. They fuss over trivial things—like telling you what to say or how to act. Ironically, what these kinds of unnatural expectations can lead to is an inauthentic workforce.

Most organizations have a mission statement, value statement, and principles they use to develop a certain kind of culture. They define acceptable standards of behavior within a company and the organization's values. Most standards are very rational definitions of good and honest ways to interact with one another in the workplace. However there are also unofficial norms not listed in the

## What is Authenticity?

Here are a few of my favorite descriptions of an authentic person:

- "Not false or copied; genuine; real."[3]
- "Representing one's true nature or beliefs; true to oneself or to the person identified."[4]
- "Being actually what is claimed."[5]
- "The extent that [a person's] conduct towards others accords with what [the person] truly believes in."[6]

organization's values or principles. They are often discussed one-on-one from mentor to mentee, at quiet lunches with no one else listening. These norms are present, but rarely openly discussed. The problem starts when these unofficial norms conflict with who you really want to be. That is when the war on your authenticity begins.

I know about working in a place where I couldn't be my authentic self and how it impacted my integrity. I was in administration at a major healthcare system for 10 years. Many consider it to be the best healthcare system in the world and I wholeheartedly agree. However, healthcare organizations are at great risk of developing an "excessive culture." By excessive, I mean a culture that excessively values one group of employees over another. In the healthcare system I worked in, that meant sometimes choosing to keep doctors happy over doing the right thing. I think this tends to happen in healthcare systems, because doctors gain so much respect for returning people to good health and they also generate large amounts of revenue for the systems. Where I worked, this led to a culture where the doctors could do no wrong, even if it meant bending the rules.

One of my issues at that healthcare system was about certain purchasing decisions. Some purchasing decisions were based on ego and lacked financial justification. When I tried to debate the wisdom of a purchasing decision, idea, or plan, different peers and leaders strongly discouraged me from debating with doctors. A former colleague shared a similar story to mine—something that's not atypical in the healthcare setting. He was called into his boss's office and told, "I heard about your disagreement with Dr. X. You were right and he was wrong . . . but never forget, the doctors are always right here. Don't do that again." There were many times when debate was encouraged in the system where I worked, but it was also discouraged. A number of discussions ended simply because of someone's job title. I struggled with the decision-making process there.

These examples show that it's not always easy for us to completely be ourselves while also conforming to cultural norms. When cultural expectations push you to go against what you know is right and what is best for the company as a whole, then I believe they go too far.

Those are the moments that force you to make an ethical decision, one that may not be too popular in your culture. What kind of decision would you make? Would you go along with the norms to keep most people happy, even if it is detrimental to your company? Or would you make the decision that aligns with your core beliefs, although it may challenge the directives of certain colleagues? It's not an easy decision to make.

## The CULT in CULTure

One reason why it's not easy to make decisions that go against cultural norms is that we all want to belong, to be accepted within our communities of colleagues, friends, families, and neighbors. Conforming helps us gain respect as recognized members of that culture. Conformity is important,

## Cultivating Common Sense

Part of being genuine is having common sense. But there isn't just one form of common sense—it comes in many forms. There's common sense in business, raising a family, fixing things around the house, and so on. Some believe that you either do or don't have common sense, but that is a myth in my opinion. It can be a natural gift, something you're born with . . . and that perspective is to some degree true. But we can overcome the lack of a natural gift by learning. You can gain common sense through study and repetition. We can learn how to be handier around the house from practice, trial, error, and watching how-to videos online. If we don't try, we cannot improve. The same is true for common sense. It is something that can be developed and cultivated.

I would pick something that you have always wanted to get better at, are not very knowledgeable about right now, and work hard on it for a while. It can be something personal, a hobby like woodworking, or something more work-related, like negotiating. Then as a dear friend of mine, Bojan Bajić, who lives in Sarajevo says, "Try and then learn. Try some more and learn some more."

helpful, and necessary for a society to function, but some of it is absolute poison for people who are different in a beautiful and harmless way. It's led me to think about the word itself—ever notice that "cult" is in the word "culture"? There is a reason why.

People join cults to feel like they belong somewhere, are accepted, and protected. The norms within that cult may be very different from society as a whole, but its members change who they are in order to belong. While a cult is an extreme kind of social group to belong to (and usually has a very negative and unhealthy dynamic), people want similar things from their broader culture. They want to belong in their society, feel safe, and be accepted by others.

Cultures also have expected behavior patterns that may seem harmless on the surface, but which may be harmful to some in the long run. There are many wonderful aspects of every culture. However, most every culture has a little bit of cult in it. The negative side effect of all this is that cultures, whether at work or in our personal lives, can interfere with us being who we are, and encourage us to act in ways that do not align with our beliefs.

Yet, if you want to act with integrity, you need to stay true to yourself. You have to go all-in on who you are—and doing so may make you stand out within your culture. It takes courage to do so. As CEO, I was not afraid to hire people who did not fit the mold. More importantly, our management team was supportive of letting employees be who they were. We hired them to do a specific job, but months later (after

## Integrity Dictionary

**culture**
/ˈkəlCHər/
(noun)

The customs, arts, social institutions, and achievements of a particular nation, people, or other social group.

**cult**
/kəlt/
(noun)

A group whose members have a misplaced or excessive admiration for a particular person or thing.

figuring out who they were and what their strengths were) we tried to steer them into roles in which they truly fit. Finding a job that allows you to be yourself is more important than money or a good title. I would argue that you will eventually get more money and that good title if you find a job and a work culture that allows you to be yourself and plays off your strengths and uniqueness. Being in that kind of culture will help you thrive in an authentic way.

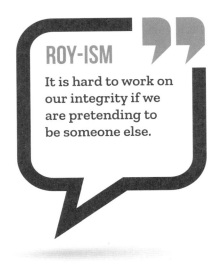

**ROY-ISM**

It is hard to work on our integrity if we are pretending to be someone else.

## Acting More Authentically

So how do you develop your authenticity? First you need to understand your core beliefs. What do you feel strongly about? What does your inner compass tell you to do? And do you listen to it? These are all questions that everyone can answer—it just takes real courage to answer them honestly. Once you can honestly assess what your core beliefs are, observe yourself to see if you act in accordance with them. Do you catch yourself telling lies? Do you say things that you don't really believe just so you'll fit in with a certain culture? Find out which actions you take that do not align with your beliefs and then start correcting them. It's just that simple. Over time you'll see some progress—your actions will support your beliefs and your beliefs will support your actions.

You can try one kind of evaluation in the "Stop and Self-Assess" exercise on pages 25–26 to take an honest look at where you're at in this process. Share it with others and use it as a tool to develop self-honesty and self-awareness of where you are and where you hope to be.

# Types of Liars

Lying of any kind is a dangerous, slippery slope. I have seen too many people start out small and end up in very bad places. Here are some of the top types of liars and the reasons why people lie. It may help you spot weaknesses in your integrity, as well as those of the people you know.

TYPES OF **LIARS** | WHY THEY LIE

| TYPES OF LIARS | WHY THEY LIE |
|---|---|
| SELF-HELP LIARS | People who lie to make themselves look better |
| CARELESS LIARS | People who don't take the time or make the effort to check what they say |
| WISHFUL-THINKING LIARS | People who lie because they want something to be true |
| PATHOLOGICAL LIARS | Often very smart, manipulative people who lie at a rate that exceeds most other liars; extremely hard to catch in a lie and leave little provable record of their lies |
| SMOOTH LIARS | Smart folks who word their lies so they can be interpreted in multiple ways; difficult to catch in a lie and often dismiss accusations as misinterpretations of what they said |
| HELPFUL LIARS | People who want to help others so much that they lie to protect them; often kind-hearted and well-meaning |
| KNOW-IT-ALL LIARS | Folks who lie to prove how much smarter they are than others; often make information up and present it as the truth |
| ENDS JUSTIFY THE MEANS LIARS | People who think that what they want to happen is so important, that it justifies lying to people to get it; have a tendency to be self-righteous |
| CHAMELEON LIARS | People who lie to fit in |
| POOR ME LIARS | People motivated to lie in order to receive an emotional response (typically pity) |
| OMITTING LIARS | People who don't tell outright lies, but omit important information that could alter another's analysis of a problem or situation |

And get some outside support too—surround yourself with happy, genuine, and caring people. People can positively influence us to be our authentic selves. I am who I am, in part, because of the people I hung around with the most. These relationships have shaped my life—they've been overwhelmingly positive and impactful. Had I not gotten married and had children, my life would've taken a very different path. Had I not hung around the most knowledgeable people in the compliance and ethics profession for the last 23 years, I would've been a much different person.

Having positive people in our lives helps us be more honest, treat others kindly, achieve more, make better decisions, and have more integrity. If nothing else, hanging around people who treat you well makes life that much more enjoyable. Seek out people with the traits you want to have—not only will you learn from them, but good integrity-filled people tend to support friends' efforts to genuinely be who they are.

Make a conscious effort to migrate toward people you admire . . . and drift away from those who might be a bad influence. Pause every once in a while to seek out some time with those positive influences. Put down this book right now and email, text, or call one of those people to set up a lunch or dinner.

Craft your actions to align with your beliefs, find a culture that truly fits you, and surround yourself with supportive people to cultivate your authenticity. It's one of the most important skills to work on to act with more integrity in your work cultures and communities.

# Q & A

## Joel A. Rogers
### on Being Authentic

Joel A. Rogers is the cofounder of Compliance Wave; he served as CEO and sold the company to Steele Compliance Solutions in 2017. Joel has traveled extensively speaking on business ethics to large corporations and government agencies and authored corporate codes of conduct and ethics for several global companies including Chevron, McCormick, and Lincoln Electric. He headed Corporate Compliance practices for UL EduNeering and RedHawk Communications, and was the director of ethics training for the City of New York; he also served on the steering committee of the Council on Governmental Ethics Laws. Joel was also named a 2008 *Millstein Rising Star of Corporate Governance* at the Yale School of Management.

Joel Rogers seems to excel at being genuine while simultaneously maintaining civil relationships with other people and respecting different cultures. Joel is an entrepreneur who's started a couple successful companies. He is also very truthful and has strong integrity . . . basically, I think he gets it. But I think where he really shines and is a good example for us all is in his authenticity. I asked him a few questions about being authentic. Here's what he had to say.

**ROY (R): I think you are more genuine than most people I have met. Why do you think I have that impression? Do you consider it a compliment?**

**JOEL (J):** That certainly seems like a compliment, particularly because I know you to value genuineness. So I'm grateful for your sharing that impression of me. Honestly, I think that your seeing me that way comes less from the way I've come across generally in conversation, and more from some very specific things I told you early on about the culture—particularly the sales culture—that I sought to cultivate at my company, Compliance Wave. Our approach is to communicate with companies about our products with unvarnished honesty, and that includes saying "we don't think this is the right fit for you" whenever we believe it. Between 30–40% of our sales calls end with us saying words to that effect.

Now, if you think I'm saying "look how much integrity we have," let me add that the primary reason we do this is for self-preservation. We do it to maintain our focus on doing the "right" business. We do it to make sure we never have conversations where someone can say we sold them a bill of goods. And we do it to maintain our reputation for speaking plainly and honestly and being people you can trust. This kind of approach has been so essential to the success of the business.

**R: Have you ever tried to help employees be their authentic selves? If so, how? Who was it and how did you try to help? Why did you try to help?**

**J:** Most of my feelings about authenticity are as much practical as they are philosophical. What I mean by that is, I think "being your true self" is defined by some important ethical and spiritual dimensions. Yet I also believe "being your true self" is equally shaped by the crappy things that can happen to you if you speak or live in an inauthentic way. And here, by "inauthentic" I mean something like "communicating something or acting in a way that's different from the plain truth as you know it."

Here's an example: The recent process of selling my company was rich with opportunities to share with employees my views of being one's authentic self. This is because the due-diligence process that accompanies an acquisition can easily give rise to defensiveness and a certain kind of "strategic" presentation of a "narrative" of who you are and what you've done. I believe that this kind of reaction is a big mistake.

On several occasions during the due-diligence process, one or another employee would approach me and say, "They're asking for X. How should we answer this?" My answer was the same 100% of the time: "Just answer it as clearly and as honestly as possible. Look," I would say, "we are a very successful company and this other company is interested in buying us because they think we've done some things right. We also think we've done many things right. Why would we now start creating narratives about what we've done, when we can just tell it plainly?"

Of course, sometimes the issue was something that you might think wouldn't make us look as good as we'd like to look. My answer in those cases was still, "just answer it as clearly and honestly as possible." The last thing we want is to conceal some truth, or tell a half-truth, and have it discovered later. We also don't want to be purchased by a company that wouldn't want to buy us, if they knew the whole truth. That would be catastrophic.

If you tell an unvarnished version of the truth, you don't have to burn any time thinking up flattering narratives, remembering what stories you told, or keeping track of the tortured meaning of the numbers you put into spreadsheets. This is because your authentic self isn't in conflict with the artificial mechanisms you've built to try to control the outcome.

**R: Do you think most struggle with being authentic, and, if so, why?**

**J:** I doubt that most people think about being authentic at all, so in that sense I don't think they struggle. On the other hand, I suspect that many people don't realize how much effort and pain can be avoided simply by being authentic. They don't recognize the incredible freedom that can come from simply being who you are in the world, instead of trying to create a narrative of a fake self that others will approve of. So, for those people, I'd say it's not that I think they struggle with being genuine, it's that they struggle (enormously) because they are not genuine.

**R: What if anything in our culture works against our efforts to be genuine?**

**J:** Seems like pretty much everything in our culture works against our efforts to

> "They don't recognize the incredible freedom that can come from simply being who you are in the world, instead of trying to create a narrative of a fake self that others will approve of.
> —Joel A. Rogers

be genuine, though I suppose that's probably true for many or most cultures. Here are four obvious ones:

- **College admissions requirements**—which seem to ask students to become hypercompetitive performance machines, often (I think) at the expense of pursuing avenues and modes of being that would help a young person discover his or her true self.
- **Social media**—the use of which encourages people to create an idealized version of themselves for the world to view.
- **The media generally**—whose polarizing effect tends to blunt many of the nuances of thought and expression that most people naturally have. In other words, in the United States we are so encouraged by the media to identify as either liberal or conservative—either CNN or Fox News. It's easy to forget that most people—*including ourselves*—don't line up completely with just one or the other of these identities.
- **Everything related to celebrity and youth culture**—which encourages us to value pretty much all of the wrong things. It's not hard to see that millions of people have subordinated their true selves to meaningless, largely consumerist pursuits.

**R: Was there a specific tipping point in your life where you think you went from trying to conform too much to being who you wanted to be?**

**J:** I think I've always sought to be true to myself, but that's not to say that there haven't been important inflexion points along the way that have given me more information about who that self really is.

One such experience was the time I spent in the U.S. Navy. Up until that time, I had no real sense of how poorly suited I am to taking orders from others in an unquestioning way. It seems that I question most everything that comes my way, and I wouldn't know how to stop doing so.

Another example is from business, and for me it was the realization that my business will most thrive when I'm clear about exactly what we do, exactly who we want to do business with, and how to be unambiguous in communicating those things. Not trying to be things we are not—that is, not trying to be something a prospective customer wants us to be just because they have money is *radically freeing*. It frees us to focus on what's most important, and frees us from a huge amount of stress. This is the environment I choose to operate in, and that has made all the difference—not only in the success of my business, but also in the quality of my own life.

I recently read a *Forbes* article on being genuine, the "12 Habits of Genuine People" by Dr. Travis Bradberry.[7] He's the author of a great book on a related subject— emotional intelligence—and his consultancy firm provides emotional intelligence tests and training to many Fortune 500 companies. Bradberry's list makes the vague concept of authenticity a little clearer.

Take a moment to have an honest conversation with yourself by evaluating where you are in your genuineness journey. How do you fare in each of the qualities of genuine people outlined by Bradberry in the chart on page 26? Look at it and write down where you think you are on each of them.

I would consider sharing your assessment with someone who knows you well, and ask for their thoughts. And don't argue with whomever you choose—if anything, ask clarifying questions. I would NOT ask for examples. There are few certainties in life, but one is that most of us become defensive when being told we could do something a little better next time. Plan on fighting the urge to disagree, debate, or disprove what they tell you. Let what they say marinate for a while before you react. Just listen and trust them—don't argue. That way you'll be more likely to get an independent, unbiased assessment. Then do what my stepmother Dottie used to tell me to do, "Shut up and say thank you."

| Bradberry's List: Qualities of Genuine People | Your Self-Assessment |
|---|---|
| They don't try to make people like them. | |
| They don't pass judgment. | |
| They forge their own paths. | |
| They are generous. | |
| They treat everyone with respect. | |
| They aren't motivated by material things. | |
| They are trustworthy. | |
| They are thick-skinned. | |
| They put away their phones. | |
| They aren't driven by ego. | |
| They aren't hypocrites. | |
| They don't brag. | |

[List source: Travis Bradberry, "12 Habits of Genuine People," Forbes, May 10, 2016, https://www.forbes.com/sites/travisbradberry/2016/05/10/12-hab-its-of-genuine-people/#67c41786461d.]

# Chapter 2

# THE BIAS EFFECT

"If one were to attempt to identify a single problematic
aspect of human reasoning that deserves attention
above all others, the confirmation bias would have to
be among the candidates for consideration."[1]
—*Raymond S. Nickerson,*
*Tufts University Research Professor of Psychology*

From birth on, we gradually and subtly develop different
unconscious biases—tendencies to favor or reject certain things,
groups, or people over others—and these biases affect our behavior.
They're inevitable, as people have the innate tendency to classify and
categorize people, experiences, and information. These biases are
kind of like shortcuts our brains develop to make fast decisions about
what we're reading, seeing, or experiencing.

Yet the buildup of certain cognitive biases can eventually cause
great harm to your decision-making skills, and ultimately your

integrity, as they often conflict with your conscious decisions about the kind of person you want to be. Many good people suffer from various types of cognitive biases that distort their thinking and bring them to inaccurate conclusions.

Biases gradually grow like a buildup of plaque on our thinking. They inhibit our ability to gather and assess information objectively. Yet, you can develop different skills and use various tools to minimize their effects. These cognitive biases must be intentionally fought in order to make rational, balanced decisions and assessments. This chapter will give you some ideas to fight that bias buildup and the limits it puts on your decision-making skills.

## Understanding Confirmation Bias

One of the most important biases to study is confirmation bias— which leads us to favoring information that confirms our existing beliefs, while ignoring information that does not. It's a very natural and unconscious way for people to process information. Why? It's a habit that helps us quickly sift through boatloads of information, it helps protect our self-esteem by telling us we are right, and it confirms our need to feel intelligent and accurate.

When it comes to confirmation bias, the real rodeo starts with information analysis. Here's the problem: two people can look at the exact same information and come to completely different conclusions, even if they try desperately not to let bias distort their analyses. We can't make good decisions if we only emphasize some information but leave out relevant information that doesn't support an outcome

**ROY-ISM**

Confirmation bias is integrity's kryptonite.

we want. Good decisions are made when we look at *all the relevant information.*

## Overcoming Confirmation Bias

Psychologist Tom Stafford believes one theory why people have confirmation bias is that their thinking is shaped by factors that motivate them—such as their jobs, backgrounds, or circles of friends. He calls this the motivational theory. We dismiss others' opinions with phrases like: "'You just believe what you want to believe,' or 'He would say that, wouldn't he?'"[2] In this case, it seems that separating their motivating factors from their thinking would help them eliminate their biases. Another theory of why confirmation bias exists is that we fail to ask the correct questions about the information we gather or our own belief systems. Stafford calls this the cognition theory. If this is the case, the way to correct the bias would be to find ways to adjust our thinking. Stafford adds, "We assume people are already motivated to find out the truth, they just need a better method."[3]

Researchers have studied how confirmation bias works too. One landmark 1979 study conducted by Psychologist Charles G. Lord and his colleagues, *Biased Assimilation and Attitude Polarization: The Effects of Prior Theories on Subsequently Considered Evidence*, used a persuasion experiment that tested the motivational and cognitive theories of confirmation bias.[4] Lord showed two sets of evidence to

> ## Integrity Dictionary
> **confirmation bias**
> /kɑːn.fɚˌmeɪ.ʃən ˈbaɪ.əs/
> (noun)
>
> The tendency to interpret information by finding or understanding information in a way that is consistent with one's existing beliefs or theories. It is a biased approach to making decisions, mostly done unintentionally, that often results in inconsistent information being ignored. People often process this information in a way that supports their beliefs, especially for highly important or self-relevant issues.

a group of people who supported the death penalty and a group of people opposed to the death penalty. One set of evidence showed that the death penalty deterred murder and should continue, while the other set of evidence showed that the death penalty did not deter murder and should be abolished. Each group accepted the evidence sets that confirmed their prior beliefs. In fact, the opposing sets of evidence seemed to only strengthen their prior beliefs. Essentially, *the study participants saw what they wanted to see.*

Then Lord's team repeated the study, but this time tested two sets of instructions along with evidence of the effectiveness of the death penalty to deter murder. One set of instructions was motivational: it asked participants to look at the evidence as if they were judges or jurors, and consider the evidence as impartially as possible. The other set of instructions was cognitive: it asked participants to ask themselves "at each step whether you would have made the same high or low evaluations had exactly the same study produced results on the other side of the issue."[5] In practice, this meant that participants had to look at the results of a piece of research, imagine the opposite results were found, and then analyze the study's methodology. The researchers called this the "consider the opposite" approach. It was kind of like instructing the participants to play the devil's advocate.

The results were astonishing. Using the motivational instructions, the researchers found the same results as the original study: participants biasedly weighed the evidence. Those who were pro-death penalty thought the evidence supported the death penalty. Participants opposed to the death penalty thought the evidence showed it should be abolished. Even though they wanted to make unbiased decisions, that didn't change the outcome of their decisions. But the cognitive set of instructions had an entirely different result. Participants overcame their biases when evaluating the evidence, and did not rate evidence that supported their prior beliefs as being better than evidence that opposed their prior beliefs. It showed that when given a thought strategy, people can overcome their confirmation bias. It showed that bias is like a wall. It can stop us if we try to go straight through it; but with another thought strategy, *we can climb right over it.*

# Thoughts on Integrity:
# Bernhard Günther

In a 2017 interview, Bernhard Günther, former CFO of the German electric utility RWE, spoke about why conquering cognitive biases is so important in the decision-making dynamics of a business. After analyzing their decision-making processes, RWE started seeing the cognitive biases affecting them:

> What became obvious is that we had fallen victim to a number of cognitive biases in combination. We could see that status quo and confirmation biases had led us to assume the world would always be what it used to be . . . We also saw champion and sunflower biases, which are about hierarchical patterns and vertical power distance. Depending on the way you organize decision processes, when the boss speaks up first, the likelihood that anybody who's not the boss will speak up with a dissenting opinion is much lower than if you, for example, have a conscious rule that the bigwigs in the hierarchy are the ones to speak up last, and you listen to all the other evidence before their opinion is offered.[6]

What was their solution to the biases affecting their collective decisions? They now encourage managers and employees to be mindful of their cognitive patterns and require a list of debiasing techniques used to evaluate any major proposal put before their board. They also encourage an atmosphere where some level of conflict is acceptable, allowing employees to feel more comfortable dissenting with an idea or decision. And Günther added, "when making big decisions, we now appoint a devil's advocate—someone who has no personal stake in the decision and is senior enough in the hierarchy to be as independent as possible, usually a level below the executive board. And nobody blames the devil's advocate for making the negative case because it's not necessary for them to be personally convinced; it's about making the strongest case possible. People see that constructive tension brings us further than universal consent."[7]

# Other Biases That Affect Decisions

Besides confirmation bias, many other kinds of cognitive biases affect our decision-making processes. Here are some other important ones to be aware of when evaluating information:

- **Affinity Bias:** This is the tendency to get along with others who are like us. It is easier to socialize and spend time with others who are similar to ourselves. This can influence us to make decisions based on emotional connections, rather than facts.

- **Anchoring Bias:** This bias comes from being influenced by the first idea presented, clouding our thoughts about latter ideas. Some people don't want to process a lot of information when making a decision. So they latch onto the first logical idea they hear and then build their position around it. It's kind of a "let's get this over with" approach.

- **Attribution Error Bias**: We tend to try to find someone to blame when something goes wrong. It's a bias that focuses our attention on blame, rather than how to fix the bad situation. It takes us away from finding an objective solution and making the best decisions possible.

- **Champion Bias**: When you value a leader's viewpoint more than factual information, you're falling into champion bias. This prevents you from fully evaluating an idea or decision. Over the course of my 17 years as CEO, this happened to me all the time and *I did not want it to happen*. People do this because they want to follow their leaders no matter what, or they are afraid their leaders will be offended by raising the new information. This is why building a trusting, open culture is very important. Bad decisions are made when relevant information is ignored.

- **Groupthink Bias:** This bias is what we fall into when we want to conform to, or are afraid to disagree with, the majority's decisions or thoughts. And that majority decision or thought may simply be the view of the most vocal person speaking up in a group. It can cause irrational and problematic decisions, as it limits the information and opinions offered before the decision is made. This bias might also cause us to repeat some things we don't necessarily believe, and may lead to negative ethical and moral consequences.

- **Optimistic and Pessimistic Biases**: These biases result from your general outlook on life. Both can alter your perception of reality and result in making unrealistic decisions based upon your unrealistic viewpoint.

- **Overconfidence Bias**: This bias results from thinking you know the answer before hearing all the information needed to make a balanced decision. Taking too much stock in your own thoughts may cloud your ability to objectively gather information. It can lead to making bad decisions and taking unnecessary risks.

- **Self-Serving Bias**: When you take credit for positive outcomes, but blame outside forces for negative outcomes, you have a self-serving bias. People with this bias seek out information that serves their purposes. They may make unethical decisions because of it. This is a very common and negative bias. This bias may lack the most integrity of all biases. Wanting stuff from other people—whether it be money, power, or influence—may be one of the greatest motivators for bias. If you only knew how much this interfered with your integrity, you would do everything you could to drop this bias.

- **Sunk-Cost Bias**: If you've already invested a lot of time or money into a project or decision, you may want to continue with it even if it's unsuccessful and you know there's a better way to accomplish your goal. This is called sunk-cost bias. People are reluctant to lose or admit they had been wrong. But being stuck in a sunk-cost bias can cause you to lose even more money and time, and may never lead you to your goal.

# Better Research

In addition to the "consider the opposite" approach to fighting confirmation bias, you can fight biases by adopting better research techniques. I have worked around people who are flaming rock stars when it comes to unbiased investigations. If you want to go all-in on fighting bias, I would suggest reading a book on conducting proper research. There is a process to it, and like Lord's study showed, new methods and processes are roadmaps out of bias. We have to fight bias with a multifaceted approach to gathering and analyzing information. Here's an abridged version of how to conduct proper research:

- Commit to using reliable sources of information (such as scholarly articles or books, trade and professional articles or books, and news from well-established newspapers or media sources), not just anything you can find on the internet.
- Search for information with unbiased key words. Instead of using search words like "autonomous vehicle problem studies," just search for "autonomous vehicle studies."
- Don't question or discount the motives of reliable sources.
- Gather all the facts, not just facts that appeal to you.
- Select key pieces of information from your searches. All information is not equally important.
- Realize that any information you find will contain bias to some degree. Being able to recognize biases will help you better decipher the information you gather.

## Bias Awareness

Spotting bias can be very hard to do, but it is an essential first step to properly deciphering information and making good decisions. If you find yourself becoming defensive or passionate about something, know that it is probably time to start thinking about how the other side sees something. Take the opposing view for a while and explore how others see an issue. After you impartially research all the facts, then, *and only then*, take a position. If you really want to impress someone you disagree with, try to explain their perspective to them. Ask them to listen to you and correct you until you can accurately represent their perspective.

Fighting your biases will help you achieve and maintain an integrity-filled perspective. It's essential to making balanced and informed decisions, whether in business or your daily life. Doing so will lead you to better outcomes for your future. Start your work with the "Consider the Opposite" exercise on pages 42–43. See what changing your thought process can do to fight your biases. Bias awareness is just the beginning to making better decisions, putting you in a better position to succeed at work and in life.

# Q & A

## Gerry Zack
### on Fighting Bias

Gerry Zack is the CEO of the Society of Corporate Compliance and Ethics & Health Care Compliance Association (SCCE & HCCA). He has more than 30 years' experience providing preventive, detective, and investigative services involving fraud, corruption, and compliance matters. Prior to joining SCCE & HCCA, Gerry was in the Global Forensics practice of BDO. He founded his own fraud and compliance risk advisory and forensic accounting firm in 1990 and operated that practice for 20 years.

Gerry Zack is an expert in risk, compliance, investigation, research, and internal controls. He is certified in several professions—all of which have an element of identifying and overcoming bias. In addition to all that, he teaches workshops on bias. Gerry's personal disposition also helps him fight bias: he is civil, curious, and slow to anger . . . all traits that help anyone wage a fight against bias.

**ROY (R): Tell us about the "reverse proof" technique.**

**GERRY (G):** Reverse proof is an investigative technique whereby a hypothesis (allegation) is proven by investigating and ruling out all alternative hypotheses. In essence, if certain signs point toward an individual having engaged in an improper act, an investigator considers all of the potential honest explanations for the evidence (alibis or any other explanation that would support a conclusion of no involvement or no corrupt intent on the part of this individual). If after considering each of these honest explanations, all are disproven, the investigator is left with the conclusion that there's only one explanation that remains— the individual committed the act and intended to do so.

Reverse proof is helpful in combatting several biases, but is particularly useful in mitigating confirmation bias, especially when all the initial signs, or allegations, seem to point toward someone being guilty. By forcing yourself to look at evidence as though the subject is innocent, somewhat like a defense attorney might do, to see if the evidence could be interpreted that way, the investigator counters the natural instinct to view things through the lens of proving a case against the subject.

**(R): What do you think about affinity bias?**

**(G):** We all have affinities with individuals with whom we share characteristics—religion, race, gender, political and social affiliations and views, career paths, and many others. These affinities affect us because there is a very natural positive response when dealing with people with whom we share these attributes. This positive feeling is mostly subconscious and can certainly be quickly overturned by other negative aspects about a person, but they factor in to our overall feelings about a person. Similarly, when we have nothing in common with someone, there is a natural level of discomfort, perhaps even outright negative feelings for that person. Affinity biases affect us in many ways—from casual conversations to investigative interviews to even how we interpret documentation provided by someone.

**(R): Why do you think it is important to understand confirmation bias?**

**(G):** When we've already concluded one way about a matter, new information that conflicts with that conclusion is unwelcome. As a result, our minds do some amazing gyrations (most of which we aren't even aware of) to either dismiss that new piece of information or explain it away as some anomaly or error. Confirmation bias is the scourge of investigations. Investigators have to take extra efforts to reverse or minimize the effects of confirmation bias, since it is a natural reaction to form some conclusions from the very outset of an investigation.

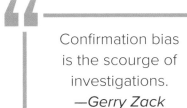

> Confirmation bias is the scourge of investigations.
> —*Gerry Zack*

**(R): How can independent advisors help us with bias?**

**(G):** An independent advisor can play the role of a devil's advocate, forcing us to consider alternatives to our current thinking. The term "devil's advocate" apparently originated in the Roman Catholic Church in connection with the canonization (sainthood) process. Once an individual was identified as a candidate for sainthood, it was the job of one person (the devil's advocate) to identify all the reasons why this person should NOT be canonized. Independent advisors can also simply provide a fresh set of eyes, taking a new look at information without prior influence.

**(R): Why do you think people see bias in others and not themselves?**

**(G):** It's simply the very nature of unconscious bias—by definition it is unconscious. We simply don't see these biases in ourselves, unless we specifically go looking for them.

**(R): What is your favorite form of bias?**

**(G):** I have no biases about bias. However, confirmation bias is the most prevalent, the most complex, and the most difficult to mitigate . . . even when we are aware of it.

**(R): When trying to understand someone, what are signs that the person has a bias?**

**(G):** It varies, depending on the nature of the bias. Affinity biases are some of the easiest to identify, since the person often exhibits physical reactions associated with either negative or positive responses triggered by this bias.

Confirmation bias can be a little harder to detect, but it also can show itself in how a person initially reacts to new information. You can often tell if the person is either quickly attempting to dismiss it, or if their reaction suggests an attempt to devalue or criticize the information rather than a "let's take a look at that" approach.

**(R): What causes biases? How do people develop them and why?**

**(G):** This would take a book to explain, and I don't have the scientific background to be able to explain it all. However, there are certainly numerous connections between affinity biases and the environments in which we were raised and our life experiences. Confirmation bias is more complex, but is also impacted by patterns of thinking we are exposed to early in life. Very importantly, the nature of our biases *does change* over time due to some of these very causes.

**(R): What do you believe is a big obstacle to fighting bias?**

**(G):** I often say that you can't eliminate a bias, but you can take steps to counter it. The biggest obstacle continues to be that people don't acknowledge that they even have biases. Once they acknowledge their existence, steps can be taken to counter them.

**(R): What are the most effective ways to fight bias? And do you think people can ever really be free of bias?**

**(G):** There are a lot of techniques, including some I've already discussed, like using an independent person to check our work or serve as a devil's advocate. Consciously reminding ourselves to consider all information, recheck our work, consider alternative theories—all of these techniques can help. Writing this down can actually help. Rather than simply thinking about alternative theories, write them down. With affinity bias, before interviewing someone, identify what obstacles to the interview might be based on the existence or absence of shared characteristics with the other person. Then, take extra effort to prepare for the interview. Finally, get sufficient sleep. Numerous studies show the many effects of fatigue. But one of the most damaging effects of fatigue is that it virtually doubles or even triples our confirmation biases. It becomes progressively more difficult to contradict our previously held beliefs as fatigue sets in. That's another reason why the statement "let's take a fresh look at this in the morning" really is good advice.

**(R): You have done many presentations on bias. If there is one thing you could get people to take away from those presentations, what would it be?**

**(G):** Awareness of and acknowledging the existence of our biases—that really is at least half the battle.

Let's practice the "consider the opposite" approach to overcoming bias. I need you to go all in on this exercise. You have to fully commit. Abandon for a moment your personal beliefs.

Pick a topic you feel pretty strongly about. It might be a political or social issue. Do not pick a topic that you are almost ambivalent about. Try to pick something in the middle of your passion continuum.

Write a paragraph describing your perspective on that topic. Note things you believe to be true that support your perspective. Provide any evidence or facts you might have on the issue. Then put the paragraph aside for a while.

**Your Perspective**

_____

_____

_____

Now search for information about that topic that supports the opposite perspective. Search for professional surveys, research studies, or scholarly articles written by respected individuals. Write the key reasons you find others have for taking the opposite perspective. Then write a paragraph supporting the opposite perspective. This is where you have to fully commit. Go all in. Pretend if you have to. Be passionate if you can. Include a quote or two from an article that supports the opposite perspective. Share some data from a survey or research if you can.

## The Opposite Perspective

_____

_____

_____

Now compare your two paragraphs. Look at both. Think about how you felt while writing the opposite perspective. Think about how you feel about your perspective now. You may not have changed your mind, but do you feel more informed? Do you think you will change the way you describe or defend your perspective on the issue in the future? Do you feel like you have done something positive? Do you see or feel any bias in your first paragraph?

**Option 2:** Try this exercise with a colleague or friend. Evaluate one another's paragraphs. Can you help each other see some of the biases in your thoughts?

You'll notice that recognizing bias does not guarantee that you will change your mind. Practicing bias awareness is not intended to change your mind . . . _although it might._ The purpose of bias awareness is to be a more effective critical thinker who makes well-informed decisions.

# Chapter 3

# THE TRUTH AND CIVIL DEBATE

———

"Don't raise your voice; improve your argument."[1]
—*Desmond Tutu, Human Rights and Anti-apartheid Activist*


"In all debates let truth be thy aim; not
victory, or an unjust interest."[2]
—*William Penn, Quaker Leader and Political Activist*


In 2016, Oxford Dictionaries declared "post-truth" the Word of the Year. They define it as: "relating to or denoting circumstances in which objective facts are less influential in shaping public opinion than appeals to emotion and personal belief."[3] Some people associate post-truth with politics, but it has a much broader application. This word exemplifies a problem that goes way beyond politics and which seeps into our daily interactions with one another. A post-truth era eats away at society's integrity.

According to *Forbes*, "the old adage was that we lived in an age of 'information overload.' Now we're dealing with '*mis*information overload,' says [neuroscientist and author Daniel] Levitin. It's easier, he says, to make a webpage that looks as authentic as a real news site like *The New York Times* or *FORBES*. Years before such pursuits were tougher: cranks churned out their missives on basement printing presses, easily identified by the smudged or crooked type . . . Viral untruths get even more credibility now with millions of likes and re-tweets."[4]

All this misinformation can lead to some heated, yet misinformed debates between people. How can we hear each other and get to the truth in these moments? Levitin thinks it's important to "get humble. 'If you have humility, you're open to learning . . . If you think you know everything, it's impossible to learn. So approach new claims with some questions. "Who said so?" "What's the evidence for it?"'"[5]

## What is Civil Debate?

Levitin's thinking is at the core of civil debate. Civil debate is when two or more people sit down and have a discussion after which both parties feel as though they have had a chance to make their points. In a civil debate, people feel as though their ideas have been seriously considered by others with opposing viewpoints. No one feels as though they have been personally attacked in a civil debate. It allows us to dissect information, ask questions, and hear things we may not have heard before. In really effective civil debates, participants think of things neither side has considered before.

Getting to the truth is often very hard. We need help and thoughts from others. Some of the most evil times in human history occurred when thought was repressed and people were shouted down. We should all do our best to help debate become more civil with our fellow humans.

I've come up with some principles of civil debate, designed to help you practice this way of communicating your opinions. These principles will help you stay engaged, remain calm, and refine your argument. But civil debate is not just about playing nice—I want to win every debate I am in. *Feel free to want victory yourself.*

**ROY-ISM**

**Personal enlightenment and civil debate are inextricably intertwined.**

### Principles of Civil Debate

Try one or all of these tactics next time you enter into a civil debate:

- Before debating, describe your opponent's position to them until they think you have it right.
- Take joy in your opponent's ability to make a good point and tell them when they do.
- Take a break or ask to meet another time if either one of you becomes too frustrated.
- Avoid questioning motives, assume your opponent's disagreement might just be a lack of understanding.
- Use their disagreement as a seed of an idea to refine or clarify your point.
- When your opponent causes you to change your mind about an element of your position, tell that person.
- When your opponent wanders off from a good point he or she has been making, help steer the conversation back to what was originally being discussed.
- Occasionally ask your opponent to repeat what he or she has just said. This helps you listen to what that person has to say and buys time to formulate your next thought.
- It's easier to disagree with things you understand than things you don't understand, so *ask lots of questions.*

- Periodically start a sentence with, "So, what I hear you are saying is . . . "
- Smile—or at least make sure you're not frowning or showing concern.
- No debate should start without ample time to conclude it calmly. Never finish a debate in the heat of the moment.
- Do not debate in a place where your opponent may be uncomfortable, such as in public places.
- If other people complicate the civility of the discussion, stop.
- Have empathy for your opponent, particularly if debating is not their thing.
- Get background material. Ask for something to read that will help you better understand that person's viewpoint.

I am all for making your point in a debate. Share all your facts and evidence. Be passionate. Care deeply. Be forceful. Disagree all you want. Just do all that civilly when you debate, and the truth will have a greater chance of making an appearance in your life.

## The Cancel Culture

One reason why it's so critical to ensure civil debate is alive and well, is because of what's become known as "cancel culture." This is when people are "canceled"—shut out from media, cast away from social and professional groups, and ignored or dismissed—for expressing questionable opinions and opposing viewpoints, or for their criminal or unethical actions. It often happens to celebrities or other famous people. Their "canceling" is a form of boycott, which limits or eliminates their ability to work and reach the public. The "cancel culture" can put limits on what people feel comfortable saying publicly, and it can unfairly condemn people. It's a quick judgment that doesn't allow others to learn and grow from their mistakes as well.

This canceling and judgment is sometimes warranted, such as when people express bigoted or racist remarks, and we have good laws against hate speech. However, some people use this logic of "protecting people" to block the speech of people they simply disagree with. There are countries where people fear for their lives if they have publicly disagreed with their government. Their culture got to a fork in the road and justified banning speech and thought for whatever reason, and ended up oppressing people.

President Barack Obama described part of the cancel culture problem and its impact on civil discourse and social change best at an October 2019 Obama Foundation Summit:

> This idea of purity and you're never compromised and you're always politically woke . . . you should get over that quickly. The world is messy. There are ambiguities. People who do really good stuff have flaws. People who you are fighting, may love their kids and share certain things with you. And I think that one danger I see among young people, particularly on college campuses . . . I do get a sense sometimes now among certain young people, and this is accelerated by social media, there is this sense sometimes of: "The way of me making change is to be as judgmental as possible about other people, and that's enough" . . . That's not activism. That's not bringing about change. If all you're doing is casting stones, you know, you're probably not going to get that far. That's easy to do.[6]

Leaders like President Obama are standing up to the problems limiting honest and integrity-filled civil discourse—such as the cancel culture phenomenon.

## Listening is Critical

Listening is a critical component to breaking down the barriers to having a civil debate. People who have different views may have done their research too. If we don't listen, we cannot learn what others know. When we make an incorrect statement, other people can help us consider other viewpoints. If you really want to make a better argument, you have to listen to others to understand how your argument is being perceived.

My work on this book is a great example. The whole editorial process has been like a back-and-forth debate. My editor Karen tells me where the gaps are in my thinking and in how I explain my thinking. In some cases we just disagree about how to think about something. But 90% of the time, I smack my forehead and realize I did not explain myself clearly. By listening and revising, my writing becomes better, my arguments clearer, and my chance of getting my thoughts across to other people better. The benefit of listening is not just to hear evidence that will change your mind . . . it is far more often that listening will help you organize your thoughts and get your point across better.

One technique to try offers an effective way to prove you listened during a debate. Spend a few minutes in the beginning making your opponent's case. The other person should correct you until you are able to get the other person's position right. Take listening beyond just a promise to listen—prove you listen by trying this with someone. Consider trying the "Listening and Debating" exercise on pages 61–62. It may help you *really hear* an opposing viewpoint and better clarify your argument.

## Thoughts on Integrity: Shane Snow

> The best kind of debate, on the other hand, is the kind where the goal is to make progress together. The process of this debate often leads the group to explore ideas that no one member could have come up with on their own.[7]

—*Shane Snow, Science and Business Journalist for* Forbes, Fast Company, The New Yorker, *and more.*

## Take the Civil Debate Challenge

Like anything, if you want to get better, you have to practice. I suggest you practice listening to and repeating another person's viewpoint. Commit to a day or a week of it. Make it a challenge. Challenge yourself to demonstrate listening to whomever you talk with that week. Don't try to figure out if you are in a debate or a conversation, just listen. You have two simple rules for this period you commit to practice—don't share your view and engage only in their views. With practice, you will become more accustomed to debating in a different way—first understanding another's viewpoint and then sharing your viewpoint.

The next time you get into a debate over an idea, start with this technique and see how much more civil it is even after sharing differing ideas. Lots of people talk about listening, but few actually commit to active practicing. Be different. *Do more than say you listen.*

You'll find that it's ok to disagree, but there is an art to disagreement. A good debate helps you get to the truth. And knowing the truth about an issue will move you toward making better decisions.

# Q & A

## Dan Roach
### on Civil Debate

Daniel R. Roach, JD, oversees the compliance function for Optum360, a healthcare revenue cycle technology and services company. He's on the board of the Society of Corporate Compliance and Ethics, and is a past President of the Health Care Compliance Association. In addition, Mr. Roach has contributed to several books and  publications. He has also served on the audit committee of two large healthcare systems and an insurance company. Dan is a frequent speaker on the topics of compliance and business ethic programs, tax-exemption, Stark law, and governance issues at board and management meetings and seminars around the country.

Dan was on my board for many years. As CEO I appreciated his ability to support me when I needed it and civilly explain to me why I was wrong when I was wrong. Truth be told, Dan doesn't really say you're wrong, he keeps as much of your perspective as possible and enhances it to get you back on the right track. He rarely ever raises his voice. He doesn't use a lot of words to explain his perspective. He doesn't talk unless he feels a real need to, so when he speaks people tend to listen. On the board, Dan typically only talked when the discussion was at an impasse. He waited until everyone was a little exhausted and had started to repeat themselves . . . or in other words, when our board was stuck. He figured out solutions that gave both sides more than they asked for, and eliminated untenable things. On the whole, both sides came out better even though they had to give up something. I have never met anyone more effective at civil debate.

**Roy (R): Do you think society is struggling at the moment with civil debate and getting to the truth? If so, why?**

**Dan (D):** Yes to both. With regard to civil debate, I believe that a number of factors have contributed to what I perceive is a decline in civil debate. One factor, in my view, is the growing tendency to dismiss people as "horrible" and therefore unworthy of respect because they have different views than we do. Unfortunately, the list of things that puts people on the "horrible" person list seems to be growing. What at one point was a much shorter list of largely criminal behavior seems to be morphing into anything you do that I would do differently—from eating habits to political views and lifestyle choices; to views on guns, abortion, immigration; and the list could go on and on. While you may have other points of view or make different choices than I make, these differences should never be big enough (in my view) to overcome the need to treat people with dignity and respect.

Technology exponentially exacerbates this problem. I can now **convey a response** at a rate that is much faster than my ability to thoughtfully **communicate.** First, email and social media allow (and condition) me to instantly respond, without the benefit of reflection about the content or impact of my message. The consequence is frequently short and poorly constructed responses which frequently do not accurately convey context. Second, social media has given us the remarkable ability to express our views to a much larger audience instantaneously. Historically, when I said or wrote something stupid, unkind, or thoughtless, it was largely limited to the unfortunate few in earshot or my intended recipient.

Another contributor is the ability to communicate anonymously. Instead of Dan Roach, I can be CmplyKng93 and say whatever I want with little fear that what I say will get back to me. Anonymity allows people to be crueler, more demeaning, and more thoughtless than they would ever be in person. These different factors allow us to immediately and widely deliver thoughtlessly generated content.

All of these factors may only be symptoms, however, of the underlying problem, which is that we don't value others nearly enough. Of the many things I enjoyed about working for Catholic Healthcare, one of the most important was its position on the inherent worth of every person. As individuals, we might have polarized viewpoints, but a viewpoint was never enough to deprive people of their value as human beings with inherent value and rights. A society that dehumanizes people ends up with people who do not behave humanly. In my view, we need to be less focused on our status and more focused on what we do to build others up, which is why I have long argued that the two most important words in the English language are "I'm sorry."

Getting to the truth is more difficult when our agendas or status in life are linked to whether or not others agree with our viewpoint. On the flipside, getting to the truth is much easier if I check my agenda at the door, am willing to listen, and treat others in the room with dignity and respect, regardless of whether I think that they deserve it or not. But I do want to clearly concede that I have much room for improvement. I still find myself regularly wishing I would have been more thoughtful, understanding, compassionate, and forgiving, and less concerned with being right or winning.

**(R): What does it mean to have a civil debate?**

**(D):** In my view, civil debate is nothing more than keeping your cool under pressure or when engaging with someone who has a different point of view. You can listen and respond politely and thoughtfully even though you may disagree (or even strongly disagree) with another's position or perspective.

I would also note that being civil is not the same as surrendering your point of view or backing away from your beliefs. In some cases, we *may* change our minds if we listen carefully. Or we can agree to disagree. We can thank people for their input and perspective, even when we decide to choose a different path. We can make hard decisions (and even decisions that leave others unhappy) without being mean or arrogant about it.

I've experienced how civil discourse can help

> " Getting to the truth is much easier if I check my agenda at the door, am willing to listen, and treat others in the room with dignity and respect, regardless of whether I think that they deserve it or not.
> —Dan Roach "

us move through difficult moments. A number of years ago I was in a meeting with a new CEO who had walked into an organization with serious financial challenges. He came to a meeting of the legal department that was headed by the general counsel, a legendary healthcare lawyer who had been instrumental in creating the company. The CEO asked every department to cut 10% of their budget, and it was clear that the legal department was seriously challenged by this request. How could it commit to reduced costs when it did not control the flow of litigation, changes in the regulatory or enforcement environment, or labor and employment issues that drove legal costs? All fair questions, which the CEO acknowledged. The CEO expressed his admiration for the GC and department, told everyone how much he appreciated their work, and said that he knew it was a difficult request. However, he continued (in the nicest way I had ever seen) to tell the group that it needed to help their GC find the 10%, or he would regrettably have to find a GC who could. It is to this day one of the most effective examples of civil discourse that I have ever witnessed. The message was quietly and thoughtfully delivered, but unmistakably clear. By the way, the legal department put its thinking caps on and met its budgetary goals.

**(R): Give us your definition of integrity.**

**(D):** Doing the right thing even when it's hard, I don't feel like it, or it's not in my best interest, particularly when no one is looking. I may find another person's actions or point of view disappointing or even offensive, but integrity is the ability to engage in principled decision-making and behavior regardless of the other person's behavior.

**(R): What are the most common mistakes you see people make in the heat of debate?**

**(D):** Two things. First, we take disagreement or different points of view too personally. When I became comfortable in my own skin, I stopped being offended if others disagree with me. One of the great things about living in a free society is that we have the ability to make choices and hold beliefs that are different than those around us. Unfortunately, that is not the case for much of the world.

Second, we don't spend enough time listening so that we really understand the problem or the context. When I speak, I frequently ask people how many believe bribery is wrong. Typically, every hand in the room goes up. I then share the story of a pro bono client from a war-torn third-world country who in our initial conversation asked me how much we would have to pay to resolve the matter. When it finally dawned on me that the client was talking about a bribe, I indicated that it was not something we would do. I later found out that at one point the client's father (who had worked for the government prior to a military coup) had been briefly imprisoned. For the several weeks before his father was released, he went down to the jail every day and brought his father food. The only way he got in to deliver the food was by paying a modest bribe to the guards. When I learned this, it placed his initial question to me in a whole different context.

**(R): What role does civil debate play in getting to the truth?**

**(D):** Frequently the truth doesn't come out if we aren't willing to listen carefully and ascertain all the facts, understand the context, or understand the perspective of the participant. Facts matter. Context matters. Even perspective matters. Many years ago, an auditor came to me thoroughly steamed that a mid-level executive in the organization had expensed a rather pricey Weber Grill on her expense report. Obviously, there was no place for the grill in our office building and the audit leader wanted the executive terminated for misuse of company funds. I agreed to look into the matter. A few hours later I walked in the executive's office and after some small talk, explained that the auditor had a concern about the Weber Grill that showed up on her expense report. She laughed, and proceeded to explain to me that she had not expensed a Weber Grill. Rather, she had taken her team to a meeting in Chicago and had bought dinner for the group at the Weber Grill Restaurant. Clearly the auditor did not have all the facts.

In another situation, another auditor (by now you may understand that I read a great many audit reports) alleged that the CEO had violated company policy by renting a luxury car. After investigating, I found out that the CEO of our nonprofit healthcare system indeed rented a "luxury" car—at least the way the rental car company defined "luxury." What had been left out of the audit report was that the CEO was traveling with three other executives (two of whom were 6' 5" tall). They had been at several days of meetings in one location so they had a full complement of luggage, and needed to get to a meeting four hours away when flights were cancelled. While the car rental company may have included the Buick LeSabre in its luxury category, I have yet to run into anyone whose definition of a luxury car is the Buick LeSabre. In this case the facts were right, but the context mattered.

**(R): People talk about listening during a debate, but how can we make sure we turn it into action?**

**(D):** This was really hard for me to do, particularly since as a lawyer too much of my training was devoted to how to give answers. My advice is to say as little as possible, at least until everyone else has had a chance to talk. If you must talk, ask questions . . . more questions than you think are necessary. When you do ask questions, ask questions that are designed to elicit information, not infer judgment. If you are fact-finding, rather than judging, you might ask someone: "Can you walk me through the steps that led to this action?" In my experience, inserting value judgments rarely produces more facts and regularly shuts down otherwise cooperative participants. I frequently make a list of questions I want to ask during a meeting, not because I need answers to the questions necessarily, but because I want people to get all the information as well as their cards on the table.

Listening also has another benefit. Some people process information by talking, and if you don't let those people talk, they will walk away from the meeting feeling frustrated, left out, or worse, not bought into the decision. While this trait initially frustrated me, I finally learned that 90% of the time we would get to the right result in any event, and everyone walks away satisfied they have been heard.

**(R): Did you have a mentor or someone you looked up to because they constantly sought the truth through civil debate?**

**(D):** Several great mentors—my favorite professor in college was a person who rarely revealed where he stood on an issue until the debate was over, and he was always kind regardless of the questions or ill thought-out positions that college students like me frequently articulated. My boss early in my career was a great mentor who pushed me out of my comfort zone to help me grow. However, my shining star of civil debate is Carol Bayley, an executive at Dignity Health, who has perfected the art of asking questions, and more importantly, *good questions*. When I first started working with Carol, I was occasionally frustrated by the number of questions she asked. What I thought would be a 10-minute conversation would almost always turn into 20- or 30-minute conversations. I felt like it slowed me down and I had a lot to do. I soon realized, however, that slowing down frequently got us to better solutions. Carol not only wanted to get to an answer, she wanted to get to the right answer. Moreover, Carol taught me that how you get to the answer is frequently as important as the answer itself. Carol is a remarkable communicator who taught me a great deal!

Here's how you can practice listening and then debating civilly. Try it in a group setting. First pick a controversial ethical dilemma to discuss. Write it on a flip chart for the group to see, along with two stands to take on the issue. Try a dilemma specific to the workplace or one's personal life. Here are a few examples:

- Your manager tells you that an employee will be laid off in the coming months. You happen to be good friends with that employee, who is in the process of purchasing a new home. The layoff has many potential consequences related to that large purchase. Do you tell your friend about your manager's decision? Or do you honor your manager's wish to keep the information confidential for the benefit of the company?

- You witness a car bump into a parked car in a parking lot and the car leaves the scene. You have the moving car's license plate number. There appears to be no damage to the parked car. Do you report the incident to the police or leave a note on the parked car? Or do you forget about the incident since no damage seems to have been done?

Tell the group that each side of the room represents one stand on the issue. Ask everyone to take a stand on the issue, and move to the correct side of the room. Then, each person should explain their position. The goal is to try to convince people on one side of the room to change their minds and see the issue from a different perspective. If they do, they should move over to the opposite side of the room. If the group gets stuck, try saying or asking:

- Tell me what you just said in a different way.
- Are you saying that . . . ? [and then try to rephrase what they said]
- Ask specific questions about the topic.
- Where did you get this idea?
- Who else shares this idea and what do they think?

After debating in this way, assess the results. Which side has more people on it at the end? Who was more effective at convincing others of their position? Why? Who stayed with their original stand on the issue? Why?

# Chapter 4

# CRITICAL THINKING— INTEGRITY'S BEST TOOL

"We put too much of a premium on presenting and not enough on substance and critical thinking."[1]
—*Susan Cain, Author, Lecturer, and cofounder of Quiet Revolution*

After gathering factual information, discussing opinions, listening to others, and really being honest about your core beliefs, what is that final step in the decision-making process? Critical thinking. Thinking critically involves questioning pieces of information, being curious about ideas and issues, and admitting when you might be wrong. This kind of thinking leads to well thought-out decisions and judgments based on logic and reason. It enables everyone to act with more integrity when making decisions, and it's something we all can work on having.

Critical thinking is important in our daily lives. It helps us make better decisions about the products we buy, the jobs we choose, and the people we associate with. It's also essential in business situations.

It helps teams make better decisions and find solutions that can potentially save their company time and money. It helps managers avoid biases when making hiring decisions. It helps investigators find the real cause of an issue. Ultimately, critical thinking can lead to decisions that make companies more successful and people happier in their lives.

## A Major Test

Every decision—whether it's minute or major—is a test of your critical thinking skills. And I've been tested many times throughout my career. But I was in my tenth year running SCCE & HCCA when one of my biggest tests occurred. My CFO and his assistant walked into my office and calmly said, "$1 million was just stolen from our bank account." They talked as if they were giving an update on the status of our coffee supply. I think they were in shock. That moment began a yearlong period that can be best summed up as the worst year of my career.

Much of the information we had was a bit sketchy, but it appeared that three eastern Europeans remotely took over one employee's computer and transferred $475,000 to a state bank in Romania . . . *twice*. I later read in a translated Romanian legal document that when the three people went to the bank to take the money out, the Romanian bank employees became suspicious. This suspicion bought us some time to convince the bank that it was our money and it had been stolen from us.

Ironically, as part of the great change Romania went through after the U.S.S.R. collapsed, the government worked on improving their justice system. Many US judges and lawyers helped them set up a better legal system, and that alliance between the US and Romanian legal systems later turned out to be very important to our organization and our desire to reclaim our money. Thus began the most important critical thinking process I have ever gone through.

I immediately called our board chair to report the issue. We are a nonprofit organization and the board's immediate responsibility was to hire an attorney to investigate the possibility that staff were involved in the theft. They asked me to report the issue to the local FBI office, which I did. My responsibility was to hire an attorney to help get the money back and a computer forensic specialist to find out how the theft happened, so we could plug our now obvious IT security holes.

**ROY-ISM**

If the lack of critical thinking got you into the mess you are in, then it's likely critical thinking is what it will take to get you out of it.

I was ready to fly to Romania to talk to the bank before they released the money to someone else. However, one of the first things our attorney told me was that I could do nothing to try to get the money back. Quite often by the time people find out money has been stolen via wire transfer, the money has been transferred again and again. Because of this most people never get their money back.

The lawyer's logic was solid but it was devastating to me. I felt totally responsible for the mess and wanted to fix it as quickly as possible. I felt responsible because the buck stopped with me no matter who had made a mistake. The minute they told me the money was gone, I realized I had not done enough critical thinking about managing or questioning our IT security. I had focused on other things. My effort in IT security was inadequate and I now knew it. I wanted to fix this. I wanted to get the money back.

## Getting Our Money Back

One day, I was sitting at my desk in a state of total despair (seriously, I cannot tell you how horribly I felt). I believed FBI Headquarters could help get our money back (as they often do in these cases), and I wanted to call a connection I had there. With my attorney's permission, I called my connection and told him the story, saying, "I believe the FBI could get our money back—something that rarely happens in cybercrime cases." The FBI is a tightlipped organization that follows their policies fanatically, and as a result my connection said very little except suggesting that I call our local FBI agent. I smiled . . . I knew that's what he would say, and told him, "I already did. Thank you for your time, sir."

I felt better. For the first time I had a little hope. I was not sure the local FBI was equipped for this sort of thing. I had little faith in the bank. Meanwhile, I worked with our board's attorney, who was investigating me and working with our board throughout the whole process. As it turned out, myself and our staff were found innocent.

I spent most of my time with the computer forensics specialists, who helped us plug our IT security holes. I was tortured by the fact that I didn't think to go through this critical thinking process with cybercrime experts to develop our cybersecurity system *before* the money was taken. This is sadly a common occurrence. People wait until there is a problem and then go through an effective critical thinking process. Oddly, as was the case with me, a very limited critical thinking exercise of our IT security would have prevented the problem. With the assistance of these experts, we immediately implemented several changes to our network . . . any one of which would have prevented the problem in the first place.

Six months after the theft, my CFO and his assistant came into my office. This time they told me the money was back in our bank account. There was no email, phone call, or communication of any kind from the bank or anyone else . . . just a wire transfer to us from the Romanian bank containing all but about $18,000 of our money. Oddly enough, there was no feeling of joy whatsoever—I was still miserable about the whole thing. Then a couple years after the incident I ran into my connection at the FBI. He told me that the FBI was able to help get the money back, as it has done in many cases.

## Why Critical Thinking is Critical

The lesson from the whole process can be summed up very simply: without going through a critical thinking process and using expert advice, you might just make a mistake that costs you a million dollars or worse. Our cybersecurity system lacked integrity. As a result, some people who lacked integrity got pretty close to stealing our money. After we realized our mistake, we implemented a critical thinking process that involved many experts to solve our cybersecurity problems and protect us from future cybercrimes. It was one of the most elaborate critical thinking processes I have ever been involved with.

Experts can be key to critical thinking. I utilized the advice of several experts after the money was taken. Some of them helped me get the money back, others helped me make sure it didn't happen again. Many professionals study their area of expertise for years, take great pride in their profession, make solid well-informed decisions, and often have great integrity in their field of expertise. In addition to consulting experts, it's also important to follow a critical thinking process when approaching a problem.

## Steps to Thinking Critically

The following critical thinking process is the multi-tool for having integrity when making decisions. Keep it by your side. Review this process and you'll see how important it is to follow when making decisions. If you want to get it right with the least amount of effort, consult someone who has expertise in the area about which you are trying to make a decision. This is a tactic I've used many times in compliance when investigating an issue, but it applies to all aspects of life. Going through this process will help you arrive at a solid, informed decision. Test it out with the "Try Thinking Critically" exercise on pages 77–78.

# THE CRITICAL THINKING PROCESS

**01** Identify the problem.

**02** Gather information.

**03** Understand and review the evidence with experts.

**04** Eliminate less valuable information with experts.

**05** Summarize the remaining evidence with experts.

**06** Select key point(s) with experts.

**07** Evaluate potential decisions with experts.

**08** Make a decision.

**09** Implement the decision.

**10** Test the effectiveness of the decision.

**First, identify the problem**. Do two relatively quick and simple things before you start the critical thinking process:

1.  State what you will be researching in as simple terms as possible to narrow it down to one succinct and clear subject. The more focused you can be during your critical thinking process, the greater your chance of getting it right.
2.  Break the problem down into researchable components. Don't have one critical thinking process for a bunch of parts—have many critical thinking processes, one for each part.

**Next, gather information.** Start gathering information about the different aspects of your topic. But know that the greatest risk here is bias. Confirmation bias is poison to critical thinking. Just use some common sense with regard to what sources to use or ignore . . . and don't just gather information from a few sources. If you're not sure where to get the information, go to people you respect who have experience in the area you're researching and ask for sources.

**Now, understand and review the evidence.** The goal here is to get all the information you can before proceeding. If you can't remember a fact off the top of your head, know the research material well enough so you can easily reference it and quickly find the information you need. Being familiar with the information will lead to interconnecting threads that provide even more context to your decision. Ask experts to review the information you've collected and then discuss how they view the information and which connections they see.

**Next, eliminate less valuable information.** Don't overthink this. Just shave off information that is deemed less important by you and an expert in this area. This is a step I see people fail in the most. That is why your experts are so important. Assessing the relative importance of each piece of information is critical. Choose information from trusted sources.

**Summarize the remaining evidence.** No big deal; just get the information in some order on a sheet of paper. Review this with an expert.

**Select key point(s).** Select a few key pieces of information with the help of an expert. On occasion, one or two key facts can help you eliminate several possible outcomes or decisions. Conversely, a few key facts could point to only one or two possible outcomes or decisions.

**Evaluate potential decisions.** By now, momentum for a particular outcome or decision has been lurking around you and the experts you've consulted. You are so well informed by including expert opinions and sorting through all the facts, that it is likely this step is just a formality.

**Make a decision.** If you've gone through all these previous steps, this step is almost a no-brainer. A wonderful byproduct of the critical thinking process is that it reduces stress, because by the time you are done, you'll be more confident in your decision. When you follow a critical thinking process, *the decision is the easiest part.*

**Implement the decision.** *This is the time for action!* Make sure the decisions you make are faithfully implemented.

**Finally, test the effectiveness of the decision.** *Never, never, never* be unwilling to admit that you made a bad decision; if so, start the whole process over again.

Some people think that your decisions, statements, and actions are the keys to having and acting with integrity. Although that is true, your decisions, statements, and actions are a result of your thought process. If you want to act with strong integrity you need to make strong decisions, and if you want to make strong decisions you need to respect and use a critical thinking process.

# Q & A

## Margaret Hambleton
### on Critical Thinking

Margaret Hambleton has over 20 years' experience in healthcare compliance, including roles as chief compliance officer for large, integrated health systems providing services in multi-state regions. Through this experience she is recognized as an industry thought leader and highly sought after speaker and collaborator. She has a very well-rounded understanding of operations, having served in leadership roles in Risk Management, Human Resources, and Insurance Operations. Ms. Hambleton is currently President of Hambleton Compliance LLC, a consulting firm serving the healthcare and compliance community.

Margaret Hambleton and I have worked together for many years. We have disagreed on occasion. What I always enjoy is that Margaret never makes it personal. She makes it about the facts and information. She also is unafraid to speak her mind and disagree when she feels the need to. One of the most enjoyable aspects of working with Margaret is that when the decision-making process is over she supports what we have decided, even if it isn't exactly what she had been advocating for. She moves on to the next challenge. She is the ideal person to help work through big issues because she uses an effective critical thinking process.

**Roy (R): Do you think a critical thinking process can help people have more integrity?**

**Margaret (M):** Absolutely. I have always said that if I had one superpower, it would be perfect perception. Think how wonderful it would be to know precisely why someone is doing or saying something; to understand the motivation, context, expertise, bias, etc. Unfortunately, none of us have perfect perception. Therefore, we have two things by which we can judge a situation; assumption or critical thinking. When we rely on assumptions, we ignore the impact of our own motivation, context, expertise, and bias. How can we claim to have integrity, even when we are attempting to do the right thing or take the right action, if we don't put aside our assumptions and carefully, thoughtfully, and fully examine all the information available to us?

**(R): Are experts helpful in the critical thinking process?**

**(M):** Consulting with experts is certainly helpful in understanding the scope of the problem, evaluating gathered information, considering options, and understanding academic literature and best practices. One of the problems, however, is identifying the right experts. Many of us think of experts as those individuals with advanced degrees and special skills; the lawyers, auditors, executives, and other professionals. Sometimes we have to remember that the expert may be the clerk on the floor who is doing the work. The important thing here is that it actually takes some critical thinking to determine the right experts to provide useful insight into the question at hand.

**(R): How do you make sure that you gather information from unbiased sources?**

**(M):** You can't—there is no such thing as an unbiased source. Whether we like it or not, *we all have bias*. Sometimes it is explicit and obvious, sometimes implicit, sometimes it is unintended, and sometimes it is the product of the system the problem is being evaluated in. The closest you could come to an unbiased source is probably double-blind peer-reviewed scientific research, but unless you are a physician or other scientist, this type of source is rarely helpful with the everyday problems most of us deal with. I think the question is: to what extent can we determine that the information being gathered is reliable? That is to say, to what extent can we trust and depend on the information we have gathered? To check to see if the information you have gathered is reliable, you should see if the information stays the same over time, if the information is internally consistent and consistent over multiple sources, and whether or not others looking at the same information draw the same conclusions. Even when you have clearly biased sources and you can confirm that the information provided is reliable, you may not want to discount it.

**(R): Where else do people go wrong when gathering information to make a decision?**

**(M):** Confirmation bias is always a problem when gathering information to make a decision. *Humans love to be right.* It is often easy to seek out information that confirms our assumptions and discard information that doesn't confirm what we think is the right answer. To guard against confirmation bias, it is important to work just as hard to try and disprove your assumptions or what you think is the right answer as you do to confirm your assumptions.

Another thing that can go wrong is failing to modify the plan as you gather more information. Often, we start off with a robust plan about who we will talk to, how we gather and test information, and who we involve in making decisions. It can sometimes be really tough to modify the plan, even when we know that the plan is no longer effective. We just hate to change course.

Finally, I think that often we don't do a very good job at defining the problem. Many times, we jump into fact-gathering without actually knowing, in very specific terms, what problem we are trying to solve. When we don't define the problem well, we can't determine what information is or isn't important, or we end up addressing the symptoms rather than the cause of the problem.

**(R): We don't need the name of the person, but please describe someone you know who has remarkable critical thinking skills. What do they do differently than others?**

**(M):** I worked for someone once who was infuriatingly good at asking questions. He could connect dots that to me just didn't seem to be connected. Now, I hate feeling that I am not prepared. Before meetings with this individual, I would pore over the information I had gathered and think about what information I might still be missing, how the information is connected, what else might the information be connected to, and who else might have information that could contribute to decision-making. Without fail, during the meeting he would ask a question I had not considered. It was not just that he was one of the smartest people I ever met, but he could always see where the potential holes were. Even when there were not holes in the information, his questions always helped me be able to defend the decision with facts and data.

**(R): Why do you think it is so hard for us to revisit a decision we have made, admit we were wrong, and make an adjustment?**

**(M):** I think the problem is that we tend to frame the question as one of "right" and "wrong." Just because a decision is made that doesn't solve the problem or is not as effective as we would like, doesn't mean the decision was wrong at the time it was made. No one likes to be wrong . . . and many will actively fight to prove they were not wrong. If we don't think of a decision as wrong, but instead as an opportunity to learn more about the problem, it may not have the same judgmental connotations and make it more palatable to make adjustments and move forward.

**(R): Do you think people in general have abandoned critical thinking skills?**

**(M):** I don't think that people have abandoned critical thinking skills, I think they just haven't been taught these skills. When people think about the discipline it takes to critically think through a problem, they may think that it will take too much time, energy, and resources. While it might be counterintuitive, utilizing critical thinking skills and techniques generally gets you to a good decision much more quickly and efficiently.

**(R): I believe that our collective integrity has hit an all-time low, people are fed up and the pendulum will swing back to a period of reason. Do you share this view?**

**(M):** No, I don't think our collective integrity has changed much over time. There are certainly people who will lie, cheat, and steal; there are people who refuse to listen to any argument that doesn't support their position; and there are people who believe that anyone outside their "tribe" is somehow out to get them or less worthy of consideration. This has not changed, but what we have now is social media amplifying their troubling views. Our public discourse has certainly become more disturbing and, I hope, will swing back to more reasonable discourse. That said, I believe that the vast majority of people are people of integrity. They have good intentions and work hard to do the right thing. We see, time and time again, people willing to bring problems forward and working collaboratively to help solve those problems. What we need to do is figure out a way to amplify the good work of most people and the positive impact they have on our work and in our communities. By doing so, we will see our collective integrity continues to be strong and that doing the right thing is more rewarding than the alternative.

> "I believe that the vast majority of people are people of integrity. They have good intentions and work hard to do the right thing.
> —*Margaret Hambleton*

Practice thinking through a problem using the critical thinking process. Here are some problems you can try working out using critical thinking skills:

- Select something you have considered buying personally. The more complex a purchase or cost the better. Make a note of the best idea you have of what to purchase right now without further analysis. Save it for the end of the process. Now use the critical thinking process to determine what would be the best purchase decision. Several steps require the use of outside expertise. Feel free to use articles or other resources; however, for at least one of the "seek expert advice" steps . . . talk to a human directly.
- Look at a big decision made at your workplace, like the purchase of some relatively expensive item, a major policy change, or a new product line. If you are not currently working, think of a past job or do this for a group you are currently involved with, such as a nonprofit, church, or any other group or organization.

Now follow these steps while working through your chosen problem:
- Identify the problem.
- Gather information.
- Understand and review the evidence with experts.
- Eliminate less valuable information with experts.

- Summarize the remaining evidence with experts.
- Select key point(s) with experts.
- Evaluate potential decisions with experts.
- Make a decision.
- Implement the decision.
- Test the effectiveness of the decision.

If you are working in a group, share your results with the group. Did someone take a different route to solve the same problem as you? Did someone have an innovative way they thought about the problem?

Here are some questions you can ask about your decisions for this exercise:

- If you made a decision before starting the process, compare it with your decision after going through the process. Did you come to the same conclusion after the critical thinking process? Even if you still came to the same conclusion, do you feel better about your decision after going through the critical thinking process? And do you feel better prepared to sell others on your decision?
- Did you change your decision because of one step in the process? If so, why was that step important to you?
- Did you change your decision because of the whole process? If so, describe how the whole process helped you.

# CONCLUSION

While doing research for this book, I found people working hard to promote a society with individuals who seek truth and have integrity. I found a groundswell of growing awareness and disdain for the post-truth era. Then I had an integrity epiphany. I saw the signs of big change.

I've been lucky enough to experience two explosive periods of change in my life. I worked in the personal computing industry as it exploded in the early 1980s and got into compliance and ethics in its early years in the mid-1990s. In both cases I saw early on that, "This thing is going to be huge." And in both cases people told me, "These things would amount to nothing."

Ironically, in both cases, people who had the most experience and knowledge told me I was wrong. The information technology community told me personal computing would amount to nothing, saying, "You can't put computing into the hands of the users—it will be chaos." They knew how hard it had been to program computers in the past. I completely understood their misperception. However, once they saw how spreadsheets, database management, and word processing operated in the average person's hands, they understood that big change was coming. It revealed that what they knew from the past interfered with their vision of the future.

The second revolution I experienced was in the field of corporate compliance and ethics. Once again, the experts said it would amount to nothing. The legal community not only told me that compliance and ethics would amount to nothing, they said it was harmful to companies. Then historic corporate compliance and ethics failures occurred at Enron, Penn State, Wells Fargo, and various churches . . . and the legal community began accepting compliance and ethics efforts in their organizations. They saw the value of preventing, finding, and fixing ethical and regulatory problems.

I was young when the IT folks told me personal computing would amount to nothing. I assumed the adults knew more than I did and I drifted away from a field that grew exponentially. I was there first, I knew it would be big and I walked away . . . and it's a decision I later regretted. A few years later, I made a promise to myself—if I ever saw something big coming again, I would ignore the doubters. When people doubted the start of the compliance and ethics industry, I remembered that promise. I not only ignored them, I and a few others started the Health Care Compliance Association and the Society of Corporate Compliance and Ethics. Together they are now the largest organizations of their kind in the world.

I see a third explosion of change coming. I think honesty, integrity, and the truth are coming back to the forefront of society. My hope is that this book will help that movement. I believe readers who use some of the tools and skills I suggest will begin acting with more integrity. I wrote this book in part because I saw so many very bright people who I trusted say things that were not true—not because they were malicious, but because they were biased, weren't being authentic, could not debate effectively, or skipped the critical thinking process. The thoughts and exercises in this book can help.

People are flawed, but with awareness and conscious decisions to pursue a life filled with integrity, we become better every year.

The change is slow. Some don't immediately see the improvement. Sometimes you have to look a little further back to see how far you've come. Humanity is a constant work in progress . . . and so is having integrity. My advice is to keep up the progress, do the work, and just watch your integrity grow.

# FURTHER READING

Here are some of the top books I recommend for learning more about critical thinking, investigations, civil discourse, honesty, ethics, and integrity.

**Ariely, Dan. *The (Honest) Truth about Dishonesty: How We Lie to Everyone—Especially Ourselves*. New York: HarperCollins Publishers, 2013.** Duke University Professor of Psychology and Behavioral Economics Dan Ariely researches decision-making processes and behavioral economics. In this book, Ariely discusses what makes people cheat and be honest, using results from his research and experiments.

**Bloch, Meric Craig. *Workplace Investigations: Techniques and Strategies for Investigators and Compliance Officers*. Minneapolis: Society of Corporate Compliance and Ethics, 2013.** Meric Craig Bloch is the vice president of Global Investigations for Booking Holdings and the author of three books on workplace investigations for the

Society of Corporate Compliance and Ethics. His book *Workplace Investigations* covers techniques and strategies that investigators and compliance officers can follow to conduct a thorough investigation into allegations of misconduct at their workplace.

**Dalio, Ray. *Principles: Life and Work*. New York: Simon & Schuster, 2017.** In investor and entrepreneur Ray Dalio's book, he covers the principles that have made him successful in work and life, including the importance of thinking independently, finding the truth, and being open-minded.

**Gentile, Mary C. *Giving Voice to Values: How to Speak Your Mind When You Know What's Right*. New Haven, CT: Yale University Press, 2010.** Author Mary Gentile is a professor of practice at University of Virginia-Darden School of Business and a consultant on management education and values-driven leadership. Her book, *Giving Voice to Values*, encourages leaders to act on their values even when facing opposing pressure using real-life business examples and social science research.

**George, Bill, and Peter Sims. *True North: Discover Your Authentic Leadership*. San Francisco: Wiley, 2007.** Former Medtronic CEO Bill George discusses how anyone can become an authentic leader by following their inner compass in this book, which includes sections on being your authentic self and practicing your values and principles.

**Levitin, Daniel J. *A Field Guide to Lies: Critical Thinking in the Information Age*. New York: Dutton, 2016.** McGill University neuroscientist and TED Speaker Daniel Levitin, whose research focuses on pattern processing in the brain, details four pitfalls in the critical thinking process in this book, warning readers about misinformation in books, websites, videos, and social media, and explaining how to evaluate claims to determine the truth.

**Society of Corporate Compliance and Ethics.** *Ethics and Compliance on the Job.* **Minneapolis: Society of Corporate Compliance and Ethics, 2014.** This book is an anthology of articles from *Ethikos*, an SCCE publication focused on business ethics, which covers five main topic areas: establishing and promoting an ethical and compliant work culture, implementing an ethics and compliance program, communicating about ethics and compliance, educating employees, and assessing and measuring a program.

**Weiss, Art, ed.** *Building an Ethical Culture.* **Minneapolis: Society of Corporate Compliance and Ethics, 2018.** Art Weiss is chief compliance and ethics officer for TAMKO Building Products and faculty member of the Santa Clara University MLS in Corporate Compliance Program. In this book, Weiss gathers industry expert advice about enhancing organizational culture—from the impact of an organization's culture to techniques for overcoming barriers to an integrity-filled culture.

# SOURCE NOTES

## INTRODUCTION

1.  Marcel Schwantes, "Warren Buffett Says Integrity Is the Most Important Trait to Hire For. Ask These 12 Questions to Find It," *Inc.*, February 13, 2018, https://www.inc.com/marcel-schwantes/first-90-days-warren-buffetts-advice-for-hiring-based-on-3-traits.html.
2.  Barack Obama, "President Obama in conversation with Yara Shahidi and Obama Foundation Program Participants," Obama Foundation, YouTube video, October 30, 2019, 16:42–20:48, https://www.youtube.com/watch?v=Ioz96L5xASk.

## CHAPTER 1

1.  Steve Jobs, "2005 Stanford Commencement Address," Stanford University, June 12, 2005, https://news.stanford.edu/2005/06/14/jobs-061505/.
2.  Vinca Russell, email message to author, July 10, 2019.
3.  "authentic," Dictionary.com, accessed December 27, 2019, https://www.dictionary.com/browse/authentic.
4.  "authentic," Dictionary.com.
5.  Charalambos Vlachoutsicos, "What Being an 'Authentic Leader' Really Means," *Harvard Business Review*, December 7, 2012, https://hbr.org/2012/12/what-being-an-authentic-leader-really-means.
6.  Charalambos Vlachoutsicos, "What Being an 'Authentic Leader' Really Means."
7.  Travis Bradberry, "12 Habits of Genuine People," *Forbes*, May 10, 2016, https://www.forbes.com/sites/travisbradberry/2016/05/10/12-habits-of-genuine-people/#67c41786461d.

# CHAPTER 2

1. Raymond S. Nickerson, "Confirmation Bias: A Ubiquitous Phenomenon in Many Guises," *Review of General Psychology* 2, no. 2 (June 1, 1998), 175.

2. Tom Stafford, "How to Get People to Overcome Their Bias," *BBC*, January 30, 2017, https://www.bbc.com/future/article/20170131-why-wont-some-people-listen-to-reason.

3. Tom Stafford, "How to Get People to Overcome Their Bias."

4. Charles G. Lord, Lee Ross, and Mark R. Lepper, "Biased Assimilation and Attitude Polarization: The Effects of Prior Theories on Subsequently Considered Evidence," *Journal of Personality and Social Psychology* 37, no. 11, (1979), 2098–2109.

5. Tom Stafford, "How to Get People to Overcome Their Bias."

6. Bernhard Günther, "A case study in combating bias," *McKinsey Quarterly*, May 2017, https://www.mckinsey.com/business-functions/organization/our-insights/a-case-study-in-combating-bias#0.

7. Bernhard Günther, "A case study in combating bias."

# CHAPTER 3

1.  Desmond Tutu, "Address by Archbishop Emeritus Desmond Tutu: The Second Nelson Mandela Annual Lecture," November 23, 2004, Johannesburg, South Africa, Nelson Mandela Foundation, transcript, https://www.nelsonmandela.org/news/entry/the-second-nelson-mandela-annual-lecture-address.
2.  William Penn, *Fruits of Solitude, in Reflections and Maxims, Relating to the Conduct of Human Life, New Edition* (Manchester: John Harrison, 1839), 31.
3.  "Word of the Year 2016," *Oxford Languages*, accessed December 30, 2019, https://languages.oup.com/word-of-the-year/2016/.
4.  Parmy Olson, "Why Your Brain May Be Wired to Believe Fake News," *Forbes*, February, 1, 2017, https://www.forbes.com/sites/parmyolson/2017/02/01/why-your-brain-may-be-wired-to-believe-fake-news/#6281a9181464.
5.  Parmy Olson, "Why Your Brain May Be Wired to Believe Fake News."
6.  Barack Obama, "President Obama in conversation with Yara Shahidi and Obama Foundation Program Participants," Obama Foundation, YouTube video, October 30, 2019, 56:32—58:22, https://www.youtube.com/watch?v=loz96L5xASk.
7.  Shane Snow, "How to Have a Productive Debate," blog, accessed January 21, 2020, https://www.shanesnow.com/articles/debate.

# CHAPTER 4

1.  Susan Cain, *Quiet: The Power of Introverts in a World that Can't Stop Talking* (New York: Broadway Paperbacks, 2013), 52.

# ABOUT THE AUTHOR

Roy J. Snell is a cofounder and former CEO of the Health Care Compliance Association and the Society of Corporate Compliance and Ethics. As a former administrator at the Mayo Clinic in Rochester Minnesota, he worked in IT, the business office, and laboratories. He is the former compliance officer for the University of Wisconsin Medical Foundation and Hospital and also worked briefly for Deloitte and PricewaterhouseCoopers as a consultant in the compliance area. Roy is a frequent speaker and writer on subjects related to the compliance profession. He is currently working for SCCE & HCCA as a strategic advisor to the CEO. Roy has a master's degree in Health and Human Services Administration.